this book is

...

without it, there wouldn't be this book.

for my grandma.

In addition to this being a piece of literature by me, the first piece is written by my late grandmother. She died 50 days before this book came out. She never got to see this piece of literature to fruition. Throughout the 98 years of her life, she wrote poetry.
As of October 15th, 2023, she is officially a published poet.
...

Thou art the potter
    I am the clay.
Hold me o' lord
    To walk in thy way

Hold me o' lord
    To follow they word
Open my heart
    To believe what I've heard

I have heard o' lord
    How you died on the cross

How you gave your life's blood
    For a world that was lost.

A world that was filled
    With darkness and sin.
With sickness and death
    Among all men.

I have heard o' lord
    How in Pilate's hall
You bore the stripes
    For one and all.

That in the believer
    No sickness can stay
For Jesus the Saviour
    Has made the way.

He made it simple
    A child understands.
The way of salvation
    In the heart of man.

So create in me
        A heart that is clean
And a mind that thinketh
        No evils of men.

Then will I know
        A more perfect way
For thou as the potter
        Has molded the clay.

- The Potter ~ Amanda Morton

PROLOGUE.

they tell
ghost stories
of our youth
claiming to be warnings

our past ghosts
haunt us as shadows

our future ghosts
haunt us as
dreams

~ghost stories

I.

INNOCENCE.

not knowing you're
naive
isn't ignorance

it's childhood

~childhood

i love crayons
and markers
and dogs
and cats
and my dad
and my mom
and my sister
and my stepmom
and my step sister
and my stepbrother
and my step father
and my step sister
and my step sister

i wish i didn't have to
have two sheets
of paper
to draw my families

i find it wasteful

but
at least i get two christmases!

i'm just a kid
and when i grow up
i hope i can be just as happy
as mom and dad
are
they loved each other so much
they let each other go

that's what they say
to do in the movies at least
except there's just so much yelling
and screaming
and cursing...
why didn't they show that in the movies?
i'm just a dumb kid
that's what dad tells me
at least

when i cry
he just tells me to grow up
and be a man

if he didn't cry
i shouldn't either.

i wanna grow up to be

just
like
him.

~6

you would always sneak out of
restaurants
my concerts
our home
i would always wonder
where you were
everytime I asked the question
i got the same answer

the smell of cigarette smoke
lingered on the air
tobacco and ash
made you happier than i did
i would stand in the smoke
filling my lungs
and sticking the stench
to my polyester hoodies
i thought that if I filled
my being with
what you loved most
you would finally love me a little

~cigarette smoke smells like home

dashing through the
evergreen trees
we clutched on tight
to our hats
and broomsticks
for they made us
that much faster

the wind brushed our faces
like we were flying
through the air

our kindergarten coven
loved to pretend
that we were witches
we would squeal
laughing hysterically
as we danced around
our firepit
chanting
the song of the witches

as nightfall came
and the streetlights
turned on
we put our hats in our bags
and our broomsticks on our sides
we said our goodbyes
and put our secret lives behind us

it was the first time
i hung out with those friends.
it was the only time
i hung out with those friends.

~witch hunt

i still remember
the fall fair
the stench of the carnies
the half-broken roller coasters
and popcorn seeping
in through the holes
of my size 5 ivory coloured crocs

we would go every year
although I had to drag you
i never really liked riding
the coasters
i was always too scared
of moving too fast
and standing on
ever-shifting ground

i would love
to play games though
the ones that rip you off
on your third toss
after getting your hopes up
from the first two

i still play those games–

one time
i lost you at the fair
i yelled and screamed.

but I couldn't find you.

hobbling through the
mirror maze
i stumble into my reflection
thinking it's you

~the fall fair

4 hours

you get out of the car
blasted with cold
and the cacophony
of cracking bones
a body anxious to be moving
for the first time
in what felt like ages

you grab your stuffed animal
and run to the door
greeted by grandma for hugs
and grandpa in the recliner

the air smells thick of
cinnamon and holiday spirit
you look around
taking in the sights of the season
the christmas tree lit
the cookies on the coffee table
the stockings hung with care

5 years

you get out of the car
blasted with cold
you grab your bag
and you open the door
greeted by grandma with hugs
and grandpa in the recliner

the air smells thick of
cinnamon and fatigue
as you got older
they did too
you look around
taking in the sights of the season

the christmas tree lit
stocked with handmade ornaments from eons ago
the cookies on the coffee table
masterfully crafted by
toll house
and the missing B from
your hand stitched stocking

10 years

you wake up
to the sound of
your 6 am alarm
You walk to the kitchen
and make yourself a glass of hot cocoa
reading over the many "get well soon" cards
while you wait
you make an extra for her
but she's not thirsty.
she needs her rest.

the date says december 25th
but your brain says saturday
there's nothing special.
why is this saturday any different
you take your morning walk
and through the windows

of other homes
you see the cheerful faces
of children
being greeted by
grandma with hugs
and grandpa in the recliner
looking around
taking in the
sights of the season

you have been through the cycle
so many times
now it's just going through
the motions
 like everything else

you look around
at the sights of
the old season turned new

the 70 degrees and cloudy weather
the Half-Lit Broken Christmas Tree
the Stockings no longer
hung with care

bygone are the days
of white christmas
and rudolph
they have been replaced with
"let's get this over with"
and
"it's just another day"

you now finished
yet another year
another holiday cycle

sad.

this place
no longer
feels like home and it
no longer
feels like the holidays

not because it isn't home
but times have changed i guess
people age and so does perspective
the bird can't stay north for the winter.
...

merry christmas.

~home for the holidays

my dreams are filled
are filled with technicolor blurs
of which i call my childhood

i reconnect with those dreams
as if they were friends
i talk to them
as if they were family
and they respond
constantly
in the way that i do things

the way that i sit under trees
pretending it was the crab apple
that used to shade my duplex

the way i curve the b's
in my name
but never quite hit the line
because i have NEVER had
good handwriting

the way
i write dreamscapes in
my poetry to deal with big things
that i seemingly always
try to compartmentalize
into small bite size pieces

~crab apple tree

look at me.
look at me.
please. look at me.

i'm the kid
on the playground
yearning for attention

the kid on stage
asking for a bow

the kid at the foot
of the bed
begging for apologies

they never came

...

i feel as if i've never enough
for you

this has turned into
never being enough for myself

i wish the love letters to yourself
you call conversations
would one day be addressed
to me

i deserve it after
devoting all
my childhood achievements
to you

~returned to sender

stepping over pebbles
i run out of my tin-roofed house
with olympic runner speed

the sweat drips
from my brow
onto my xs t-shirt

i swing in my favorite tire
the earth is good
and still
and whole

all i need to worry
about is the tree giving way
and whether
i'm home for supper

praying over dinner
i feel whole
at our dinner table
and that's all that matters

~tin roof days

a child's legs
is a baby bird's
wet wings

capable of flying
but more
capable of falling

i choose to fly.

-flailing

II.

GROUNDED.

one day when i'm older
i'll plant a garden of my own
that no one will have to see

i'll watch my gardenias blossom
every morning

dew glisten off the
blades of grass
after the afternoon showers

and the ivy grow up
the brick
in the pale moonlight
...

it'll be
just me
my ghosts
and the garden
growing old together

~ivy

i fly like
a bird on his wings
over the lush yellow
plains of corn and hay
but stop dead in my tracks
from the scarecrows

ironic right.

i don't know why
but being filled
with faux life
scares me more
than anything

i fear that
one day
i'll stop dead
in my tracks
falling into the trap
covered by straw
and insecurity

i'll stare out of
the hole
wishing
i had never
flown at all

~screaming at scarecrows

drain my body of its blood
when i'm gone
slit my throat and
don't waste a drop

use this blood for something
because the sweat
and tears never worked
and this is my last chance

let my blood dye the white roses red
so the queen of hearts
can have her perfect garden

let my blood be the paint
on your canvas
for i would love to think
that i could be beautiful

let my blood be
the physical manifestation
of my pain and effort
the strain
i had to endure
for so long in silence

let my blood represent
the words i never spoke
but needed to be spoken
more than anything

let my blood be the purpose
to the soul
that had none.

~bloodspill

when all the water has
left the Earth parched
begging for hydration
and all the flowers have
lost their petals
due to malnutrition
remember that spring will come again

when a bear
prepares for months of silence
and solemn loneliness
does it expect the sun
to not be just outside
it's rocky home

when snow has fallen
like a blanket on a
tired aching body
do we think that the ground
is no longer there

if seeing were believing
no faith could be had
did the little girl
follow the late rabbit into
the dark woods
and get lost
and think
i wonder if the rabbit is still
alive

~dear self

when the morning dew
glazes the grass
orchards
and even miss mayapple's
perennials
the twinkling display
shown by the suns
dazzling beams
blind any
who dare to look at such explicit beauty

not only is the display pretty
but it's also
the nourishment for hundreds

food for all
sight for all

but
does the sly fox
dare to
slink and snake
it's way
through dark corridors
to take a sliver of
mayapples prized
blueberries

the blueberries were magical
magical indeed
many a legend say
they're the reason
the sky is blue
because their tint bled
into other facets of life
making other sights just
as beautiful as the blueberries
themselves
so the fox
slinked and snaked
till it took
just a nibble
of the blueberries

suddenly
all the food rotted away into ash
temptation and selfishness
ruined everything for all
food for none
sight for none

there's no more to do
the deed is done

the villagers wept
for days
weeks
months
until they faded way

from the sorrows
and bodies of the villagers
their carcasses made home for
flora
and their sorrows and grief
fed it all

the tears provide nourishment
for the new life
that grew
just like the morning dew
on the blades
of grass

~miss mayapple

vulnerability didn't use to
be the issue
now it's the only thing
i can't have.

i'm a flower
that's about to bloom
but is scared to be beautiful

~innocence

my mom used to have
jars to fill with her
freshly picked strawberries
to make them last
until she needed them

i applied this concept
to my thoughts and feelings
I compartmentalized them
into the jars and
stuck them on the shelf till
i needed them
but once I left them there
i could never open them again
nor did i want to

i shouldn't have ever tried to fit my feelings in containers

~compartmentalization

the sun bestows upon the
forsaken land
wonders of many kind

she bestows life
in the form of
flora and fauna
of many different
shapes and sizes

the sun brings great joy
to the land
expelling as much hate
out of the earth
and replacing it with
pure solace

but even the sun
has her limits.

even the prettiest flowers
have to wilt
someday
even the healthiest bird
has to land
for the last
time

the sun sheds her
solemn tears as she has
no control
over her creations
she created them with
no malice
and her sincere act
ended up
burning her in the end

then the sun sets
for even she needs
her rest
creator of beautiful things
big and small
has no control
whatsoever
at all

in holy matrimony
me and the sun
are wed
waiting for our supernova
to feel beautiful

let me explode beautifully.

~sunshine

i am everchanging
a product
of everlonging germination

allow to wake from my dormancy
and take to the sky
i'm ready

i promise

-germination

from whence my marble once came
laid the earth in the her solemn beauty
my body a reflection of
Gaia and her ways

molded from the immaculate conception
that is natural process
i was beautiful and whole
put on display for everyone to
marvel at

i, the statue, once loved
the attention of everyone
gawking at the beauty
i beheld

but after a millennia
marble is simply a rock
from the earth
nothing more
nothing less

i have been given a new purpose
by mother earth
she slowly broke me down overtime
and now i solemnly reside
in rocks beneath peoples feet

practical in use
ugly in perspective
i was slowly broken down
until the people who once
viewed me as beautiful and whole
now used me to fulfill their own wishes

i'm a rock
a speck in the grand sojourn
that is the circle of life

i, as the rock
has seen many the many phases
she decided to take
but each time she changed, i did too
i was reliant on her for my will
my drive
my purpose.

she has now given me a new purpose
she has sent me to the river
to lay with the fish and flora
except i do not lay
i am in perpetual motion
following the rapids wherever
they make take me
slowly getting chipped off
more
and
more
and
more
until i am polished with no imperfections

i relinquish myself to the river
i am just another pebble
the littlest kid once skipped
i no longer have self-purpose
only the purpose others
have given to me with their
vision of my purpose

i have been tumbled long enough
i, simply a pebble, only had
so much rock to chip off
before i turned to dust
and now i am
dirt
holder of nutrients for living things
to thrive and stronghold
for farmers to prosper

once a statue
beautiful and marvelous
then a rock
practical and small
then a pebble
tumbled and taken along
the ride of the river
then dirt
the birthplace of new life
and new happiness
for your purpose is never lost
only ever changing

~statuette

III.

GLASS CLOSETS.

there was so little around me
i thought it was illegal

"it"
was queerness

~midwestern representation

world class traveler
of paper towns
and ghost ridden
houses

where did you go
this time
take me with you
to see journeys unseen

i don't think
you're real

you cohabit the line
of realism
with santa
and the easter bunny

i know
you're too good
when i start hearing
the siren's call
emanating from
your mouth
and you trace
your fangs
with your tongue

you're too good
to be true
so travel far away
from here
to be a fantasy
in another weary
traveler's head

i wish to forget you existed

~paper towns

i'm waiting for my friend to arrive
as I wait outside the diner
people walk past
each with our own life stories
our own threads of fate

this passerby starts staring at me
he's looking at me up and down
he glances at my butt
he's still looking at it
he's still looking at it
he finally passes me
and whispers

"faggot"

i stay silent
just watching him
walk down the road
i wonder how many times
he's screamed that word
at himself in the mirror

i know I did.

(all i can say
is don't through stones
from inside
glass houses...
in this case,
glass closets.)

~glass closets

yearning for wiggle room
my body lies concrete fixed
in fetal position
compressed seamlessly into
the bathrooms's dusty corner

i cry tears
big enough
to fill the ocean
as our song is on
the songs melodies
that once filled my being
with your aura
now lay hollowed
stripped of their purpose
just random chords
played by another indie artist
on a guitar
she probably has named

i once loved you
but when hearing you speak
made me feel like I was drowning
when I could hear myself breathing
i knew i could no longer
linger here anymore

once my safe space
now a forgotten memory
joy used to live there
until it got its eviction notice

joy misses you
but i don't
she still asks about you
and i say
who's he?

~eviction notice

is the reason why you cry
every morning
because you regret what we did
in the night?

i can't love someone
who refuses
to fully love me

(i love you
like how the sun
loves the moon
i don't care if
i never catch you
the chase is
worth it to me)

...

if it's so wrong
why does it feel so right

if i shine in the day
that does mean you can only shine at night

~DL

i'm a monster
a monster in the closet
the closet monster
you were so scared of
in your youth

but it's fine
your parents convinced you
i was fake
well i'm here

i don't bite
but i do bleed
stick your stakes
to feel content
die the martyr
to fulfill
the hetero
savior complex

i'm a vampire
sucking
at your bone marrow
i have a hunger
for
blood and garlic
that'll never be satisfied

put me down please
sedate me to no return
kick me in the closet
till i'm bruised
and burn me at the stake
till i'm charcoal

i'm not enough for you
or myself
let me recluse
and be the closet monster
no one wants to acknowledge

hide me with
the tee shirts
you hang
like many of my brethren

with the socks
used to fill shoes
that leave an imprint
on my soul

the trinkets
you collect
to remember

the memories as small
as grains of sand
in the hourglass
of your lifetime

but remember this
when walls become closets
closets become homes
and homes become nonexistent
we shall still exist
no matter rain or shine

for we are not monsters
but humans
of flesh and blood
waiting to break
out of the mold
and learn to fly

flowers
bending towards
the sun
waiting to blossom
and be whole again

~closet monster

you pluck
my heartstrings
from a-g
making
heart wrenching
chords exist
may my sounds
bring you pleasure

~our love song

sometimes I daydream

...

i daydream that we're both
sailors
exploring the rocky seas
of each other's hearts
we stumble across
mermaids that look
like past lovers
islands that look like past homes
and messages in bottles
that sing songs
of love and heartbreak

...

make a map of my heart
so i can find more love
to give you when
i can't find anymore

~cartographer

take a deep breath
it's time for your first day
of middle school
your mom tells you
to make good choices
so you do
because you don't
have any other reason
to yet

...

one week in
you start changing
adolescence is slipping
from your fingers
as you start to grow
hairs on your knuckles
your pits
your back

you start looking
for a "babe"
as you dad always described
to "make yours"
as your dad always explained

...

one month in
you're not having luck
until you turn the corner

boy.

you meet eyes with
boy

boy is hot
boy is grungy and edgy
boy is everything

but why?

you're not gay?

it must just be a phase
middle schoolers are so stupid.

...

2 months in

you're still focused
on charlie
charlie is boy's name
as you found out

you've now accepted
your identity
from inside the
glass closet
and you're ready to come out

...

"we already knew?"

...

3 months in
your adolescence
has completely fleeted
it's in the ground
"where you should be fag!"

you decide to come out
to your mother.
she says she loves you
as you sob on her bed

...

4 months in
you feel like a criminal
committing identity theft
as your mother
tells you it's a phase

you're waiting out
the storm
when you are the storm
you're the problem
with no solution
the little gay boy

who's forsaking god
and is preparing himself for damnation

...

6 months in
you think about your dad
how he asks
about the babe
you've made up to
appease the beast
you don't know what to do.

you sit and stare
at the wall
expecting it to give you answers
to questions still unknown
you stay up at night
for your dreams
of living a happy life
with charlie
has turned to nightmares
where the wedding photos
have been tossed into the flames
at your crucifixion

trial by fire
hosted by your father

10 months in
the gig is up.

months of babes
turning into bros
at every corner you turn

you come out
to your father
at 12
(the ending is exactly what you think.)

he burns
you at the stake
in the name of catholicism

what a concept
to grasp at
12.

~12

list for the donation center:

letterman's jacket
cross bracelet
KJV bible, new, in box

~atheism

IV.

GILDED MONOGAMISM.

licking lips
that aren't mine
i ask
is this intimacy?

~blind

i view myself
as 2 different people
living in the shell
that transports me from
one place
to another

first:
the real me
the me that wakes up

the one that goes to work
to pay my rent
the one that drinks tea
every morning
because he refuses to sleep
the me that cries after sex

second:
the actor in me
the ghost in the shell
the one that never comes on time
the one that floats
on the night air
through apartment doors
and window sized city scapes
the gift of company
for an hour or two
the gift of a sex toy
that lives and breathes
and is yours to play with
until you grow out of it
and donate to the secondhand store

sex

touchme

if my skin is warm
is that as good as consent?

if my skin was cold as ice
would it make a difference.

...

i don't know if it would.

if i wasn't fuckable
would I have purpose?

insincere vulnerability

plunge your right hand
into my back
dance your fingers
up my spinal cord
till you reach
the trachea

grasp it
and toss me
around

i'm your ragdoll
the plaything to use
i wish to speak
your words
like a ventriloquist dummy
no mind
to worry about simple things
just a slave to your words
and thoughts

crucify me with your will power
till i submit to bloody murder
with pleasure

...

i submit to bloody murder
  to please you.
(just)

-trachea

my body
is scarred from
your touch
greasy signatures
from your hands
litter my body
and nothing makes
me feel clean

~imprint

as much as you're
the problem
am i the problem?

was i wearing the right thing?
was i being indecent?

i wish i could tell
the difference
between you and me

everything is a two way street
but i don't think it is this time

you drove on the one way
and i'm under ~~the car~~ you

~two-way street

drawing a map
of my body
we search for buried treasure

first we draw
a line
from the bow of my lip
to my esophagus

you push in
then out
in
then out
deeper and deeper
but not finding anything

we draw another line
from sternum
to pelvis
we touch every crevice
leaving no rock
unturned

we follow the arch of my back
all the way to my tailbone
and make sure i know
where x is

i feel as if
i'm nothing
without these little
x's on myself

little x's everywhere
i'm being
strip searched
for treasure
when it's all
in the eye
of the beholder

~little x's everywhere

my body is scattered
fragments of my most vulnerable self
spread all over the place
i still think about them
and wonder how they're doing

~naked

i wish i could say
better about sex

i really do

but if you bat zeros
for so long
i guess you
can't win the ball game

...

i really hope
one day
i can hit all the bases
and feel like
i scored

after everything
i feel like
i deserve it.

~the big ball game

one day
i wish to make
sounds of pleasure
and enjoy it's symphony

i don't know
what that'll feel like
but i think i will
when the time is right

even broken clocks
are right
two times a day

~broken clock

V.

MATERNAL INSTINCTS.

drunken dazing
unadulterated rage
crimson palm prints
on the bathroom walls

if i didn't have you
to clean up
the mess you made of me

i wouldn't know how to do it myself.

~maternal instincts

if i could drink the
air you breathe
the glass would be
half-empty

~pessimism

i was never the outdoorsy type

but i was that august day
when i dug tunnels
as large as the canals of venice
to make sure my mom's tears
didn't flood the town

i left town in a hurry.

to me, i was an adult
a graduate of adolescence
ready to take steps
into the real world

to her, i was a baby boy
a graduate of kindergarten
fumbling aimlessly
into walls
upon walls
upon walls

funny isn't it?

the way we think we're both right
when neither truly knows the answer

she sees the world in black in white
i see it in color
but it doesn't matter
when on the page

you both see 2+2
equaling five.

~mathematicians

drinking milk from a
coffee cup
to try and not feel
like a little kid

they say you don't know
true heartbreak
when you're young
but it felt like it
when i was beating on the
windows of the car door
screaming for air
when the button
was under my fingers

i feel so immature for letting
you affect me
but i've never been sorry
for letting myself be vulnerable

~sippy cup

affairs
of the heart
and mind

little mistakes
i dot on you with
projections
of my inner workings

if i didn't spend so much time
trying to fix you
i would enjoy you
for who you are

~savior complex

i cried to you for help
you just stared blankly
collecting each tear
you gave them to the Ocean
claiming she needed more water

~brick wall

you are the water
i need to live
droplet by droplet
molecule by molecule
i cannot escape
this innate need
for h2o

i wring your words
of their meaning
only to find a few droplets
for your words mean nothing

you actions show
you're a desert
while you scream
you're an ocean

i wish i didn't need water
because i can no longer
find it in you anymore

~deserted

i get so worried about
the small things
"my shoes are dirty"
"my nose is too big"
"my eyes are lopsided"
and it hurts when
the bigger things ache
even worse

nowhere has felt like home
in a long time

i'm still that small child
calling for their mom
after they forgot him
in the store

i can no longer find home
at least not for very long

home is where the heart is
but i hate myself so much
that i give it to other people
to let their heart beat a little longer

i give myself to others when
i can't even find a
steady pulse

i give myself to others
to try to find a home
but i can't build a
stable foundation
the structure comes crashing down
into a pile of rubble

suddenly
i have
no heart
no home
just a cavity in my chest
and tears in a pool
on the floor

~stability

if i had a flower
for every time
i wished you would treat
me better
i would have a garden

i would fill it with wildflowers
they're your favorite
even reveling in my
suffering
i think of you

i wish to make a
flower garden
out of my femininity

it has been widely regarded
as my weakness
when really
it's my strength

i have no childbearing parts
but i believe i have
the capability to mother a child
of my own

...

growing up with all women
taught me many things

I. love manifests in many forms

buying you the right cake
from walmart
on your birthday

pressed flowers
inside letters
until they're preserved
beautifully for years
to come

a baby
of which
you share a name
and features with
that you call
one of your own

II. children are as much independent
as they are an extension of your right hand

a popular belief
in spirituality
is your right hand
gives

a baby's small hands
that can barely wrap around
pinky might as well
be melded to your hand
with veins
and blood since you're made
with the same parts

in the bible
they say that eve
was made with half
the rib of adam

a baby
of flesh
blood
and
bone
weasels it's way
into your rib cage
as it has made a sanctuary
for itself
inside your heart

one day
they'll grow too big
for this cavity
and you'll feel
a hole in your chest
a baby bird
will take to the skies
floating and falling
shedding your ribs
and growing it's own

they'll need it
soon enough.
for their own offspring

III. i want to be a mother

the resilience of my mother baffles
me
i stand alone
on a precipice
and that's built off the
rib bones
of my mother

i would give my father
an honorable mention
but there's nothing
honorable there

i wish to be as strong as my mother.

to hold a growing weight
as large as a boulder
in my chest
until it suddenly flies
out and leaves me empty

she signed up
for this
and i'm eternally grateful

i wish to give myself
to a child one day
to give myself
fully to the baby
in the sling
i'll give her the best
picket house life
she could ask for
and i won't regret it a bit.

~motherhood

one day
you'll realize
i was always good enough

while i wait for that day
i'll realize it myself

~i don't need you

VI.

FATHERHOOD.

screaming into the abyss
i hear echos of laughter

you scream
at me for
answers
unattainable
and my lips stay sealed

i hate how much
we're alike

your genes
cursed mine
and my children's
 I will
never forgive you.

there's something
so solemn
about your words.
you beg
for pity
but you take
pride in
burning bridges

i hope
you smell
the smoke.

i hope it
reminds you
of home.

and i
hope you
remember
that it'll burn
till all your bridges
are gone
...
i'll never feel bad
for you.

~burning bridges

the last person i truly believed
loved me was the one
that convinced me
no one else did
and for that
i'll never forgive myself

~i loved you more.

we all had water
you drank all of yours
in a fit of gluttony

your solution to dehydration
was poisoning the water supply
if you suffered
everyone else had to as well

~you hated to suffer in silence

i took a shower
to clean myself
of you
but the bar of soap
keeps slipping from
my fingers

~dirty/i ~~can't~~ don't want to let go of you

ante up
the game has started
the objective set
win at any means necessary

i give you my finger
as the ante
you're in the game now
you can play

you're in the heat
of the game
confident in your abilities
you ask me for more
i give you the hand
it's not enough
i give you my arm
we barely scathed by for this round

you're bluffing out
the competition
but at what cost
i recklessly give myself
to you
but you can only
see red now

you approach the end
all bets are set
the game is almost through
you won
you got the jackpot
the prize
you look back at me
and i'm no longer there
just a bloodstain
in the satin seat

~gambling myself on you

when i was little
i used to try to dream
of a better life with you
i never was able to
and i always wondered why

i grew up and realized
there was no better life
with you in it
i wish I could go back
and tell him that

~sleepless nights

i long for the simplistic wonders
that life holds
through the rose coloured
glasses a child wears

i long for the moments
when we would buy
liquor store lottery tickets
and i didn't know you were
overdosing on
painkillers and margarita mixers

i still remember when
you were the superhero
in my comic book

fighting off all the evil that
came my way
when i didn't know
you were one of
the villains
too

...

the rose coloured lens
of a child
let's all the secrets
fade away
and leaves only the
technicolor world of
superheroes
cookies
and daily power ball

when you grow older
the rose glasses are
ripped from you
and you can no longer
escape the truth

dads become monsters
grandmas become addicts
and martyrs become
heathens

i still remember all the
good too
the childlike wonder of
the rose glasses
and every day
i wish i could turn back time
to get a second pair

~nostalgia

i take no shame
in calling satellites
shooting stars

when no one's
giving you hope
sometimes you have
to give it to yourself

~satellites

while i find myself
rather nostalgic
when i trip
over your
fishing line traps
thinking of you

it's fleeting

there was this time
we got stuck
in a snowstorm
before opening season

i was freezing
so you gave me
your cig scented
coat and
it smelt like home.

i loved you
so warmly
that it melted
the ice

i wish you could
have done the same

brash statements
from myself
undermine
your efforts

you showed your
love in many
interesting forms
i can't say
you didn't
think outside
the damn box

you used to love
me in the way
you used to buy
bug juice from
the gas station
for me
along with the
tall order of
fake tobacco jerky

it was my favorite
because it was your
favorite

you used to love
me in the way
you belittled
my mother
in the name of
martyrdom

you used to love
me in the way
you kicked out
my stepbrother
for being queer
so i wouldn't be queer

can't say you didn't try.

you still love me
eternally
in the way
you've passed
your blood
into my veins

...

it's the way
mom sees
you in me

i have your eyes

the ones that
pierce through
people
till they submit

i have your shoulders

the ones you could
turn cold
on a whim

i have your charisma

the one that convinced
me you loved me
for all
of my childhood

when others tell
me how bad i am
they tell me about
our traits

one day
i'll bloodlet
this curse
out of me

thank you
for my
childhood
when i didn't know
better

but now that i do
i don't need you

if i wanted to feel alone
i would stay by myself
i know better
and better is without you
...
love you dad.

~fatherhood.

i hope you like the view
from your island paradise

you're trapped there for good

-burned bridges

VII.

MELANCHOLIC.

carve a space in yourself
for me to curl up in
to feel at home

~sadist

one day
when we
settle down in
a bed of
our own
i won't feel bad
about my last name
because i will have
taken yours

release me
of my surname
service
the birthright
curse
of which i was
handed

~marriage

you were my everything
i don't mean that in a good way

...

while you were the
sun
on my cloudy days
you were simultaneously
the clouds
the torrential Rain
and the oncoming funnel cloud
just over the horizon

will i see you
everytime
the seasons change?

~consumer

i cleaned the house
of your things
i didn't want
your stench
to cling onto
my clothes
my home
my life
anymore

i couldn't bare to return them
to your house
to see your dog
daisy mae
paw at the door
welcoming me inside
with a childlike innocence

i burned your things
i watched it go up
in flames
i took in my last
breathe of you
and exhaled
what was left
out into the night air

i wish I could say I didn't regret it.

~watching you go up in flames

phantoms downstairs
from the ghosts we always kept
they love to linger around still
even after you left

they enjoy the trinkets
that cling to your smell
like i do

your flannel still resides
under my bed
sitting in the place
you forgot about

i haven't moved it.

i still hope that you care
about it enough to come back for it
the "ghosts" miss you

~phantoms

as i sit alone
this saturday
i stare at the corners
the cracks
the crevices
wondering when my hiding friends
will jump out
and surprise me
with a party

over time
they've slowly became
one
with the walls
speaking to me
through whispers
old texts
and forgotten voicemails

even if i threw
my own party
they wouldn't show up
but that's okay

my cat would
and that's all that matters

-kitty tea parties

grasping at Straws
i look for a glimmer of hope
the end is near
i know it is
over
and
over
my life flashes before my eyes
showing me how
it was never worth it
nothing ever was
in
out
in
out
in
no matter how hard I try
no air is ever enough

...

i wake up
my tears are nothing
but dried streaks on my face
my body knows me
better than I do
i was always grateful for that

~crocodile tears

i'll tell them
all in the morning
about my fever
and how
i mourn my
fever dreams
of you

the heat of
the sun
beats down
on your rocketship
as you fly far away
from me

i see you
everyday
in my dog
laika

we'll never look
at the
same sky
again
and
i don't know
how to
deal
with that

~dogtag

i'm so very scared
...
i'm so. very. scared.

i get this
melancholic feeling
once in a moon
that i make blue

fuck this cyclic pattern
i yearn
then
i yield

this whole limbo
of wanting more
then settling for less

why?

because
i'm
so
very
scared.

i want big things
but i'm not a big person
i never feel shorter
than when i'm groveling
at your feet like
a beggar for bare minimum

my brain screams more
while i scream stop.

i scream go
and you scream
"fuck, omg
get over yourself
do you know how
lucky you are?
i work very hard
for you
and i
and you belittle me.
you belittle me
over and over
and over
and over
and over
and it NEVER
ends
so fucking
get over it."

i get over it
everytime

cyclic patterns
of fighting
and fencing

the delicate art
of backing up when
shit gets close
to your chest
and going aggressive
at yours
when you're weak

do i take advantage
of you?

this is a question
i ask myself often
do i tell you
how i feel?

this is a question
i ask often

i yearn to tell
you
how i feel
how i love you
how i hate you
how i need you
how i-

there's no need to continue
there's a constant string of questions

i overthink these melancholic feelings
...
there's no answer
i've decided
whether clinical
physical
spiritual
extraterrestrial
this is just who i am

i yearn for more
and one day i will have more
but for now i wait
i wait for it.

i fear i'll always wait for it.

~melancholy

curses of my past
come to haunt my future

you're the only ghost
i've heard with this name
yet i see it everywhere

i smell your scent
on passerbys
and can never place it

i hear your voice
in the sounds
of strangers
and
i taste your lips
when we kiss

little reminders
of your existence
everywhere
yet i can never find you

strange.

~ex-lovers

VIII.

GROWING PAINS.

my feelings overflowed
like a bathtub
you forgot you were
filling

i felt feelings so big
it felt like they were
eating me alive
i didn't need any
more help
feeling that way

~carcass

i take three steps back
everytime i try
to grow into adulthood

i'm never mature enough
i'm not mature enough
i'll never be mature enough

i would love to say i'm tall
but in reality
i'm 3 kids in a trenchcoat
waiting to be called an adult

if i got a fake id
would you believe me

~3 kids in a trenchcoat

the chef prepares his cooking utensils
tonight's the night
the night he cooks the meal
to conquer all

first, he chopped me up
into 10 equal slices
then he shoved me into the oven
at 345
i baked until I was
nice and brown
then I was served on a silver platter

at the dining table
the guests patiently awaited
for the meal of their lifetimes
when it came out
they ate a little piece
then more
then when they got full
they felt bad for the chef
so they kept eating
even though their body
rejected the thought

the curtain rises
the audience applauds
and gives a standing ovation
for tonight's play
i played all the parts
i tortured myself
and called it a masterpiece
i ate myself until I was bones
and still
no one was satisfied
but the audience

~the art of performance/glutton for punishment

you kill me
over and over
and
over

...

and over

...

you bury me
but i'll always come
back from the dead

i'm different every time

soon you'll have a mob
surrounding you
of
blurred faces
who all know your name
but you still won't know mine

~blurred faces

clutching onto a bottle
2 becomes
4 becomes
6 becomes
8

i used to always
count by 8's
when overstimulated
It felt like the
only thing stable
in my life

wasn't the ground
wasn't the sky
but a number
an imaginary number
i set meaning to
because I don't believe
the ground
will stay still
while I prance
around in a
temper tantrum

i clutch onto the bottle
2 pills becomes
4 pills becomes
6 pills becomes
8

hopefully
after the
counting's done
i won't see
ground or sky
ever again.

~O.D

i can't change
i'm a creature of habit
/
i'm always changing
i'm always
unrecognizable
to my mother

if i uphold traditions
while changing every second
maybe someday
i'll be recognizable

~changes

talking to shells
of who we used to be
if i carved inscriptions
on the inside
would our ancestors
worship you like
i did

words that weren't
meant for you
will soon lay liquor laiden
on my lips

spew your
melancholic symphonies
i dented the tubas
and stomped
on the flutes

don't make a peep
or they'll think you're
out of tune

i carve out
my insides
every day
for
someone new

hopefully the
kids to come
will find my shell
and fill me with
their innocence

~make me whole again.

i would do anything for you
what do i have to do
to receive the same treatment?

~reciprocation

how do you tell your mother
you want to die

you don't want her
to blame herself
but you can't say
it's your fault
because you're her baby
starting to crawl

...

how do you tell your mother
you tried dying?

she'll blame herself
for not doing enough
but you can't say
it's your fault
because you're her baby
just now learning
to walk and smile

and what do babies do?
scream and cry
till they get attention

my attempts at attention
are attempts at my life
addictive attempts

...

it's addictive the feeling
the floating
the falling

the flatlining.
imagine if your
heart stopped beating
in your chest

you get addicted

why?

your genes

this is an unsolveable problem
it's a terminal illness
i'll soon die of.

i'm just a baby who wants to die
how could i know though
i've barely lived

i'm only 15

-15

please let me stop changing
let me stop stretching my skin thin
to make it fit
please stop time
turn back the watches
all at the same time
time travel is possible
we just have to believe

...

here i go
rambling like a child
i really need to grow up
and get over these growing pains.

-growing pains.

IX.

STARLIT DAYDREAMS.

body in heart
heart in body
let my body be the shell
for the heart that will
carry me home wherever
my love decides to flow

~home Is where the heart is

falling in slow motion
autumn leaves take
residence in the smooth breeze

our home has its windows open
airing summer out of it's walls
and drying the floorboards
of our seaside adventures
from the coast

time shifted so fast
soon snow will fall
and freeze the walls
into an ice cube
staying frozen till it
thaws out for summer

~reminiscing on sand castles

rolling cigarettes
in the old
high school
parking lot
reliving our childhood

we hazily
identify
the ghosts
of our past
in the smoke signals
we emit
from off our
tongues

will we find
answers
as long as
we keep breathing?

-high school chainsmokers

when the autumn leaves
fell and crinkled
beneath the sneakers
of kids
jumping into leaf piles
You said I reminded you
of the falling leaves

they were so vibrant
and fell like shooting stars
or down feathers off a
landing swan
i never saw that part
of myself
but to you
it shone brighter than anything else

now we're riding in the car
wondering how time could have
flown by so fast
and you're reminding me that
winter is fast approaching
as autumn is swiftly
fleeting

god. i wish moments
like this
would last
forever.

~blipping

watercolor blurs
of my 2nd grade art class

i paint pictures of
pinks, purples
but mostly the
blues

the days my dad would be
late to pick me up
smelling of smoke

the days my mom
would make spaghetti-o's
for dinner

watching fireworks
on july 4th
wishing they would
send the town
up in flames

i keep those memories
in corner of
my closet
along with
many other things

-watercolor paintings

we found a house
we can hopefully turn
into a home
i have my doubts
but I can hide
them in the
walls
floorboards
closets
attic
never to be seen
until we
inevitably tear down
this house
of shifty foundation

~foundation issues

it's such a curse
to be youthful

fingers twinkling
along the thin edge
of festering
and fleeting

this love
of joyful
abundant youth
that is festering
inside your body

this love
of joyful
abundant youth
that is fleeting
as you age

is it better
to live
or to leave.

i ended that
with a period
because you don't choose
they happen simultaneously
not exclusively

what a beautiful curse
is living.

~ youth

sand between
my wiggling toes
reading on the beach
a book with
salt-soaked
pages

daydreams of
cape cod
fly away
on a whim
of reality
breathing
in the
thick ocean air

you look over
at me
and hold my
head in your palm
and suddenly
we're home

~cape cod

i get lost in my daydreams
they float and falter
on my consciousness

i lack focus
i lack drive
i'm lacking

i'm an emotional masturbator
deriving pleasure
from procrastination

...

i live in these daydreams
they allow me to escape
from hell
when i'm forced to punch
the ticket

i look at the smoke signals
in the clouds
and they tell me how to live

sometimes i don't know
how to live by myself
so i have to rely on external sources

...

i have daydreams of you
living nightmares
in full conscious
where i see you possess
people who are "you"

people who answer the phone
in a unique way

people who grab coffee
where we used to
last fall

people with a voice
like an angel
who treated me
like a devil

...

i daydream everyday

dream is used loosely
but you have to speak
softly on things
so they get better

it has to get better.

~daydreaming

aligning ourselves
with the sun
we become
the heavenly bodies
in the night sky

dancing on
stardust
we see the future
ahead
we scream
chants of dreams
and spells
for we are invincible
in this moment

we shine as bright
as any star
because we have
starlight
living in the back
of our mind
waiting to use
our heart
as it's home

we shine our light
on others
and toss care
to the wind

we need not care
unless its for each other.

~starlight

X.

CLOSURE

little loose ends
all around
the seams
of my bust
my hips
my thighs
my skull

i was sewed
by a starving artist
who died
in the middle of making
me

i tie the loose ends
into bows
to provide
pretty closure
to their
unfinished business

-little loose ends

i didn't get to say goodbye
i don't know how i'll ever get closure
it's almost like this pit in the my stomach
is the closest i'll get
i only think that
because i'm used to closure
tasting like emptiness.

-goodbyes

i'm not looking for a
knight in shining armor
to save me anymore
i can save myself
i don't need rescuing
i didn't ever need rescuing
it just sometimes sounded nicer
and easier than what
was happening

~damsel

if i were to die
would i finish my se

i feel inconclusive
i feel like i can never
commi

pinky promises
i keep to myself
are all that matter

others would rather
lose their hand
than admit
they used their pinky
to commit to something
as silly as myse

-inconclusiv

this house's walls
still echo your
voice
whispers in the hall
screaming in the kitchen
i never thought they would
go away

i used to live by myself
until I learned to live
with person in the mirror
it made our house
feel more like a home

life got easier
when I wasn't seeing
a different person
everytime I looked in the
mirror

~self reflection

memories and thoughts
slipping through my fingers
if it's not tangible
was it ever real?

-hourglass

after their passing
i knew I couldn't live there anymore
i had to see something new
be something
do something
anything
i tried unique carpentry
i made a house of cards
but don't take me as a fool
the cards are reinforced
to be pretty
but not vulnerable

you visited again
just like how you did
that fated day
you huffed
puffed
and threw your hissy fit
trying to knock down my
house of cards
You perceive me as a Joker
but I perceive myself as
the king of the castle
or rather
my house of cards

you were unrelenting
you stayed
night and day
waiting for it all
to collapse in on me
as you've seen happen to others
you finally left
and I realized
i could be as vulnerable
as house of cards
but as strong
as a brick house

~pov of the pig

shaking hands
and faking smiles
i make apologies
work whenever
possible
you're no longer
friends
you're just people
i used to know

i see your history
and your face
but i can't place
your name

~apologies.

i'm a bird
floating and falling
flying through chemtrails
and cigarette smoke signals
finding his way home

...

i'm here now

in the new apartment
in the new life style
in the new life.

i've reached the end
of my adolescence
grains of sand
from sun-bleached days
on the beach
have slipped through
my fingers.

i'm out of time.

...

i'm now 18
without a clue
in the world

i'm a baby stumbling
around on his bird legs
waiting to grow wings
and fly far from this place

over the scarecrows
over the fall fairs
over cape cod
over martyrs and addicts
over brothers and sisters
of days gone past

…

i'm flying.
i don't have wings
but i choose to fly

i've written poems about being
a bird
the sun
a ghost.
all this time
when really i'm human
i may not have wings
but i fly through

people
places
time

i've been trying to reach the future
shedding the skin of my past
in the body
i'm living in presently

am i snake shedding it's skin
or a butterfly molting
to become beautiful

both are acts of

change.

change yourself then change the world
that was always the mantra we were taught

if i change myself enough
will i be enough
can i change the world
can i be superman.

...

who am i fucking kidding

i can't change
i've been the same kid
with the same blankies
and the same clothes
for years
god forbid i don't eat
the same cake on my birthday
every year

god forbid i don't flip switches
twice till my brain says
i won't die

god forbid i do anything
that isn't like me
because people will think
i've

changed.

i have changed.
i've changed a lot actually

i age every year
and that comes a new personality
i change myself to fit that years goals
if i fail
then i change till i succeed

maybe that's why this year
i'll be consuming yet another
me till i can be everything
and hopefully in a good way

i can't keep doing this.

i can't keep

changing.

staring at the walls
you cried as i left your car

i'm now 18
i'm older, wiser
and according to the law
an adult

i'm a freak adult
this baby with bird legs
trying to pay rent.

but at least i'm flying.

i.
choose.
to.
fly.

...

that's all.

~18

i'm damaged
porcelain that has
cracked from getting dropped
bumped
bruised
abused.

in japanese culture
they have this concept
that reinforces the ideal
of fixing porcelain
with gold to show
the beauty in your
brokenness

i'm a bird
in a gilded cage
i used to be scared
to fly
but now that i see
the ground
far below
i now know
i need not
to

i'm cracked
every crevice
little pieces of me
stitched together
with pieces
and golden thread

after the events of my life
i had to give myself advice
i don't have any other outlets

the cracks in me have names
they're babes titled
by my family

they're all named briton
that's how they know me

luckily my name.
my birthright.
reinforces the fact
that i'm

not my mother
not my father
not my trauma.

while i'm cracked
i'm not broken
i used the gold
from my gilded
cage to fix myself
and now i have closure

after everything
i still choose to fly.

~closure

XI.

EPILOGUE

if my ghosts
have offended
trust it will
continue

they haunt me
everyday
with playful daydreams
filled with
addictive fathers
loving mothers
and picket fence lives
from lives gone past

they'll haunt me
forever
and i'll welcome
them gladly

~hauntings.

Printed in the USA
CPSIA information can be obtained
at www.ICGtesting.com
LVHW010544081223
765728LV00067B/1485